Commanding Your Night Season

by Madeline James

Forward

True to form, Madeline once again provides us with a deeper glimpse into the prophetic anointing through . Throughout the pages of this book, Madeline shares firsthand experience of how dreams are a crucial communication tool for stewarding our daily lives. The congruent prayers and declarations are anointed with impartation and prophetic activation for each reader to glean from. The way Madeline breaks down the revelatory realm along with providing her suspects with heavens protocol for posturing our heart to receive pure revelatory dreams is stellar in this day and age.

Operating in the spirit realm is an experienced based and learned accomplishment provided only through our relationship with the Holy Spirit. It's evident that Madeline's growth is one to be gleaned from for those striving to be nearer to the Heart of God through the night seasons. If you are on a journey for gaining a deeper understanding of how we've been created to engage with heaven through our dreams, get ready to posture yourself to receive.

There is a new generation and a new breed of Prophets arising. positions this new breed of prophetic dreamers to maintain a lifestyle of purity while operating in a greater level of discernment as an overseer of the spiritual realm.

Holly Watson, *founder of KRGO INC.*

Krgo.org

Introduction

Dreams are the language of Heaven. It has been one of the primary ways God has chosen to speak to people. God not only uses dreams to speak to believers, but also non-believers. Dreams have a way of transcending beyond our natural limitations and speaking to the very core of who we are. From the beginning, dreams have been an integral part of the story. Amos 3:7 declares, *"Surely the Lord God does nothing, unless He reveals His secret to His servants the prophets."* God is always speaking, it is just a matter of us becoming aware of how He is speaking to us. Dreams are a part of the way He chooses to speak to us.

Joel 2:28 declares, *"Your old men shall dream dreams, and your young men shall see visions."* As we get closer to the coming of our Lord, dreams and visions will increase. When we go to sleep our spirit is wide awake. The night is an invitation to explore, experience, and travel in the things of the Spirit with the Spirit of God. When you lay down things are just getting started. There has been much emphasis on commanding our days, but what about the night seasons? I would dare to say that may be more important than the day, because your night seasons set the tone for your day.

We must learn to care for the night season as much as the day. It's important we posture ourselves in the right way so we can maximize our night seasons. Just as there is a lifestyle to the day, there is a rhythm and way of life to the night. We must guard the night as we do the day. The enemy comes to steal, kill, and destroy (John 10:10) not just in the day but the night as well. The enemy wants to steal seeds of instruction, deliverance, prophecy, encounters, etc. The enemy knows the power of our night season.

I have been a continual dreamer from a young child. As I've matured, I've learned the importance of stewarding the night season. When you learn to govern your night season, you prepare a place for the Lord to encounter you and speak to you in a way that doesn't happen in the day. The night seasons are where seeds of the enemy or the Lord are planted. We see the manifestation of those in the day. If you don't like what you're seeing in the day, take a look at what is happening in the night. If your night season has been a place of torment and terror, I believe as you read through this devotional you're going to experience breakthrough and deliverance.

Commanding Your Night Season is more than just a devotional, its an impartation. Get ready to start dreaming more and see more than you have before. I encourage you to read this before you go to bed to posture yourself. As you go through this devotional, you're going to see your night season shift in a powerful way that will lead to great encounters. These encounters will empower you for the day. It is time to take back the night and command your night seasons.

The Protocol of Heaven

Posture Your Heart

I will stand at my guard post and station myself on the lookout

tower. I will watch to see what he will say to me and what I

should[a] reply about my complaint. Habakkuk 2:1 CSB

As you start this journey through this devotional, it's important to posture your heart. Posturing our heart positions us to receive what God has. As you get ready to rest and lay down for the night, make it a practice to surrender yourself to the Lord as you sleep. Jesus is the gate through which you can travel and experience things in the realm of the Spirit. The Spirit of God never sleeps. Your body may be at rest, but your spirit is wide awake and ready to encounter the Lord.

We can learn from the prophet Habakkuk in this scripture that you have to be intentional about positioning yourself to hear, see, and encounter the Lord. He made it a practice to go to the high place above the noise and the chaos so that he could see and hear the word of the Lord clearly. Habakkuk said, *"I will look to see what the Lord will say."* Often dreams and visions are an invitation to the more. Not only do we see the dreams or visions, we have to look beyond the surface of the dream or vision to really see what God is speaking. Habakkuk was determined to position himself in a manner without distraction to hear from God. May that be your desire as well as you start on this journey.

Prayer Declaration

Holy Spirit, as I start this journey with you, I surrender myself to you. I want to posture my heart to hear and see what you have to say. Teach me how to grow in the things of the Spirit, especially in the realm of dreams and visions. As I experience and encounter you in the night seasons, teach me how to command my nights and my days. I am ready to go on this journey with you. I'm all in.

Write The Vision

The LORD answered me: Write down this vision; clearly inscribe it on tablets so one may easily read it. [3] For the vision is yet for the appointed time; it testifies about the end and will not lie. Though it delays, wait for it, since it will certainly come and not be late.

Habakkuk 2:2-3 CSB

Another part to growing in the realm of the Spirit concerning dreams and visions is stewarding what the Lord shows you. A part of stewarding is writing the vision/dream down. There's something about writing Heaven's reality down in the natural. We allow so many prophetic promises, insights, wisdom, warnings, etc. hang in the in between because we've not done our job to pull it down to establish it.

By faith, we take God at His Word when He releases it in the night and we write it down to establish it. Job 22:28 says, *"You will also declare a thing, and it will be established for you; so light will shine on your ways."* As we write out these prophetic encounters and dreams, we are releasing the decrees of Heaven over our lives. God's dreams are Heaven's reality for us. There was a time in my life when I was a therapist, and I began to have dreams about going into ministry and doing something different than I was at the time. I thought I was living in God's dream for my life, but as I began to have these dreams I saw God's reality for my life.

When I began to write them down, I wasn't just writing them in a journal. I was allowing the Holy Spirit to write it and establish it upon my heart. Writing down in the day what we see in the night establishes the decrees of God upon our lives that cause His light to shine upon us.

Prayer Declaration

Holy Spirit, I commit to stewarding the dreams and visions well that you give me in the night. I will steward them by writing them down. It says in your Word that you have written eternity upon our hearts (Ecc 3:11). As I write out the things you show me in the night, I believe that you are writing them and establishing them upon my heart. I want to live in the reality and dreams that you have for me. I will write the vision so it can be established in the day.

The Pursuit

"And you will seek Me and find Me, when you search for Me with all of your heart, I will be found by you, says the Lord." Jeremiah

29:13-14 NKJV

When it comes to the things of God, it's all about the heart and pursuit- not the gifting and anointing. The Father is all about the heart. We see this depicted in different ways throughout the Bible, especially in the story of David (1Samuel 16). Samuel came to anoint the next king and thought it was one of David's brothers because of their appearance. As the prophet looked each of them over, the Lord reminded Samuel that he looks at the heart and not the outward appearance. As the rest of the story goes, David was known as a man after God's heart. May that be our prayer. David didn't always get it right, but his heart was right in his pursuit after God.

As you press into pursuing God more diligently in your night season, be intentional and persistent. As the scripture says, *"And you will seek Me and find Me, when you search for me with all your heart."* In your pursuit, it must be a whole-hearted pursuit. God is not looking part or half your heart. He wants it all. When you give Him all of you, He will give you all of Him. There will always be a reward for your pursuit when you pursue Him whole-heartedly. He said, *"I will be found by you."* The Hebrew word for found means to encounter. As you're pursuing the Lord whole heartedly in your night seasons, not only will you find Him, but you will have an encounter that will bring transformation to your life.

Prayer Declaration

Lord, as I pursue after you in my night seasons, I commit to doing it whole-heartedly. Like David, I want to be known as one who has a heart after God. I just don't want to find you in my dreams and visions, I want to encounter you in them. It's in the place of encounter that I'm transformed. You are my reward.

Ascending Higher

"Who may ascend the mountain of the LORD? Who may stand

in his holy place? 4 The one who has clean hands and a pure heart,

who has not appealed to[1] what is false,

and who has not sworn deceitfully." Psalm 24:3-4 CSB

There is a protocol or a way of proceeding in the realm of the Spirit that we must all go through. When we go around the protocols of Heaven, we open the door for the enemy to come in. There is safety in Heaven's ways. In the first few devotionals, I have intentionally focused on the process of ascending to give you a blueprint. Ascending in the things of God is not meant to be an encounter here and there, but to be given a lifetime of access. We have access to God because of what Jesus did on the cross. To ascend in the higher dimensions of God requires purity.

As much as we focus on carrying ourselves a certain way in the day, we must carry ourselves a particular way in the night. In Psalm 24, David gives us keys to ascending higher in the things of God. This can be applied to our night seasons. Purity is important to God. Purity is what gives us access, not our giftings. Let me put it this way. The more we look like Jesus and carry his character, the greater we can ascend and experience profound encounters. Purity and character matter to God. As we encounter the Lord in our night seasons, it should cause a greater desire for purity and to not want to do anything that would cause the Holy Spirit to pull back in our lives.

Prayer Declaration

Holy Spirit, as lay down to sleep, I want to ascend the hill of the Lord and go higher in the things of God. I ask that you cleanse my hands. Purify my heart. Anything in my heart that is impure, blocking, or ungodly take it. I don't want there to be anything in my heart that would cause me to be separated from your presence or encountering you in the night. I repent of any idols or false things in my life.

Seated In Heavenly Places

He also raised us up with him and seated us with Him in the

Heavens in Christ Jesus. Ephesians 2:6 CSB

When it comes to the things of the Spirit, it's important to know who we are in Christ. You may be wondering what this has to do with dreaming and your night seasons. Knowing who you are as a child of God is everything. When we don't know who we are in Christ, the enemy will try to intimidate us. At times this can show up in our dream life through intimidating or fearful dreams. In these encounters, you have the authority to rebuke anything that has come to mess with you. Often God will use encounters like this to train you in stepping in the authority you have in Christ.

It's also important to know that you're seated in heavenly places, because you have to learn to rise about the warfare. Often, we can get can stuck in the second heaven warfare where the angels and demons are fighting. When you learn to ascend and learn to operate out of being seated in Christ, your dream life will shift. You'll begin to see and dream from Heaven's vantage point. Don't allow the enemy to pull you out of character or your seat of authority onto his turf. Ascend and take the battle to the Heavenly realm where you have the advantage.

Prayer Declaration

Holy Spirit, teach me more about who I am in Christ. I thank you that I am seated in heavenly places next to Jesus. I declare I will not allow the enemy to pull me out of my seat of authority. I command my dream life to shift so that I can see and dream from Heaven's vantage point and no longer from the enemy's view point.

Peace

Governing Peace

And let the peace of Christ, to which you were also called in body,

rule in your hearts. Colossians 3:15 CSB

I'm not sure who said it first, but one of my favorite quotes is, *"Peace is the seedbed of revelation."* The peace of God is one of the most powerful and overlooked weapons of warfare. Peace is more than just being calm. It's the government of God resting upon you, ruling and reigning in your heart and mind. In other versions of Colossians 3:15 it says, *"Let the peace of God be the umpire of your heart."* What does an umpire do? An umpire is the one calling the shots. The umpire enforces the standards and rulings in a game. They decide what is allowed and what is not.

This is a picture of how peace governs in our lives. The peace of God helps to prepare and ready the soil of our heart to receive the seeds of revelation that are released in the night season. When our hearts are ruled by other things like fear, anger, sadness, lust and so on, it will reject the seeds of God in the night season. This is likened to the parable of the sower in Mark 4. The sower in the parable represents Jesus, and he has seeds of the Kingdom of God that he wants to sow into our lives. In the parable, it mentions four types of soil- the roadside, the rocky soil, the thorny soil, and the good soil where the seeds were able to take root and grow. When peace governs our hearts, it will prepare the soil of our hearts for the seeds of wisdom, revelation, knowledge, etc. to be received.

Prayer Declaration

Holy Spirit, I declare and decree that your peace is the ruler and governor of my heart. Peace be the gatekeeper of my heart. I want my heart to be a place where the seeds of God in my night season can be planted and flourish. Peace of God, remove anything from the soil of my heart that would hinder or reject the seeds of God in the night seasons. Peace, you are the umpire of my heart.

Peace of Mind

Perfect, absolute peace surrounds those whose imaginations are consumed with you; they confidently trust in you. Isaiah 26:3TPT

What rules and governs you on the inside is what will rule and govern your surroundings. What is reigning in your mind? In the previous devotional, we discussed how peace is the seedbed of revelation. When there is chaos, anxiety, and ungodly thoughts running through your mind, it will keep you from ascending in the night season. When there is no peace in your mind, it will keep you stuck in second heaven warfare. The warfare will show up in your dreams. Peace gives you access to ascend because peace guards the presence of God in your heart and mind.

Solomon tells us in Proverbs 23:7, *"As a man thinks so is he."* This is a revelation into the things of the Spirit. You can only ascend as high as your thoughts or imaginations. What do the thoughts and imaginations of your mind look like? Paul tells us in Colossians 3:15 (TPT), *"Yes, feast on all the treasures of the heavenly realm and fill your thoughts with heavenly realities, and not with the distractions of the natural."* What you dwell and think upon matters, because your mind is a gateway into the realm of the Spirit. As you prepare yourself to sleep, be intentional about what you are thinking about. No matter what the day has been like, empty your thoughts and mind and give them to Jesus. Then ask Him to begin to fill your mind with heavenly realities. The more you train and discipline your mind to meditate on Heaven's realties, the easier it becomes to experience Heaven's realities as you sleep.

Prayer Declaration

Holy Spirit, I declare and decree that as I lay down to sleep, I will set my mind upon Heaven's realties. Remove any thoughts or imaginations that are not from you. With the help of your Spirit, I choose to discipline my mind to focus on godly imagination. Perfect peace, rule and surround my mind so I can experience Heaven's realities in my night seasons.

The Place of Safety

I will both lie down and sleep in peace, for you alone, Lord, make

me live in a place of safety. Psalm 4:8 CSB

To command your night seasons, it's important to feel a sense of safety and protection in the Lord. Safety is a place in God that we can inhibit and live in. For some of you the night is not a place of peace, but of torment. If the enemy can steal your sense of peace and safety in the night, he will steal and pervert your encounters to the place where you will dread sleeping. This promise of peaceful sleep is a weapon of warfare you can use to combat nighttime warfare.

The Lord wants you to take back your night seasons. For some of you reading this, you have experienced torment, violation, or some type of trauma in the night. In the scripture above David declares, "*I will both lie down and sleep in peace.*" It's one thing to lie down, but its another sleep in the place of peace. The Lord desires for your body, soul, and spirit to be at peace in your night season. When one of these parts of you is warring against the other it opens the door to warfare in the night.

Peace and safety is your portion. As you lay down to sleep, invite the Spirit of God into your sleep. As you make this a habit, you'll begin to see a shift in your sleep. When you invite the Spirit of God into your sleep you're inviting peace into that place. Where peace reigns, the enemy cannot. "*Where the Spirit of the Lord is there is freedom*" (2 Corinthians 3:17). As you rest, imagine yourself resting in the arms of the Father in the safest place. Beloved, you are safe and protected as you sleep.

Prayer Declaration

I declare and decree as I lie down and sleep, I will sleep in peace and safety. Holy Spirit, I invite you into my sleep. Any spirit that's not of you I command it to go and leave my sleep and place of rest. I declare my body, soul, and spirit are at peace and not warring against each other as I sleep. I declare and decree that I am safe in the arms of the Father as I sleep.

Sweet Rest

When you lie down, you will not be afraid; when you lie down, your

sleep will be sweet. Proverbs 3:24 ESV

When was the last time you had sweet rest? Sleep was never meant to be a place of warfare. The enemy knows the power of the night season. The Lord doesn't just want our sleep to be good, He has ordained our sleep to be sweet and pleasant. To be sweet is to be kind and gentle. Pleasant is to be enjoyable, satisfying, nice, and pleasing. The Lord desires for you to look forward to the night seasons and see it as a place of holy communion with him. Even as your body rests, your spirit is communing, receiving, and encountering God.

I didn't always view the night as a time of communion with God. Growing up, I dealt with nightmares, demonic dreams, and torment in my sleep. I didn't realize the power of my dreams, but the enemy did. The enemy will often disturb our sleep or find ways through open doors we have. He attacks prophetic people, and those who can see, to try and shut down their gifting. If that's you, I want to encourage you to press through to the other side of what you're seeing. Ask the Holy Spirit to show you what is on the other side of that fear or demonic dream. Often the victory or what we need to receive from the Lord is on the other side of that bad dream.

Prayer Declaration

Holy Spirit, I declare and decree my sleep will be sweet. I will no longer allow the enemy to steal and disrupt my sleep. I will not be intimidated. Help me to push past my fear dreams to the other side where you are and the victory is. I declare and decree the enemy will no longer steal my peace as I sleep. My sleep will be sweet in Jesus name.

Covered

He will rescue you from every hidden trap of the enemy, and he will

protect you from false accusation and any deadly curse. ⁴ His

massive arms are wrapped around you, protecting you.

You can run under his covering of majesty and hide. His arms of

faithfulness are a shield keeping you from harm. ⁵ You will never

worry about an attack of demonic forces at night

nor have to fear a spirit of darkness coming against you. ⁶ Don't

fear a thing! Whether by night or by day, demonic danger will not

trouble you, nor will the powers of evil launched against you. Psalm

91:3-6 TPT

There will be times in your night seasons where you will go

through seasons of warfare. Do not fear the warfare and the battles that will come in the night. You are covered. Just as when you're awake, in the night the Lord has equipped you with everything you need to overcome and be victorious in your night season. At times, the Lord will allow the warfare to come because he's using it to train you in the spirit.

The enemy will try to come under the cover of the night but know that God is with you. In Psalm 18:28, David declared, *"For You, O Lord, light my lamp; My God lights up my darkness."* If you've been in a season of warfare in the night, ask the Lord to light up the darkness and expose the works of the enemy. As you go to sleep, you can be at peace and not worry if the warfare may come or not. David tells us to not worry about a thing, because He covers us and comes to our rescue. Let not your heart be troubled or anxious. You are covered in the name of Jesus.

Prayer Declaration

I declare and decree I will not fear the warfare that may come in the night. You are covering me. You have equipped with me to be successful and victorious in my night season. Holy Spirit, light up my darkness and expose every trap and attack of the enemy. I

declare and decree I don't have to worry or be anxious about the

night. I trust you. I declare I am safe and covered in your arms.

The Revelatory Realm

The Revelatory Gifts

For to one is given through the Spirit the utterance of wisdom, and to another the utterance of knowledge according to the same Spirit, [9] to another faith by the same Spirit, to another gifts of healing by the one Spirit, [10] to another the working of miracles, to another prophecy, to another the ability to distinguish between spirits, to another various kinds of tongues, to another the interpretation of tongues. [11] All these are empowered by one and the same Spirit, who apportions to each one individually as he wills. 1 Corinthians 12:8-11 ESV

When we are born again, the Holy Spirit sees fit what gift or giftings to release to us individually. Certain giftings may come easier to you than others because of the measure the Holy Spirit has given to you. I want to encourage you to not stay comfortable in the giftings already endowed to you. Press in for more. The revelatory gifts consist of word of wisdom, word of knowledge, prophecy, and discerning of spirits. The revelatory gifts are not just for the day, but they can also be activated in your night season.

Whether the revelatory giftings come natural to you or you are growing into them, ask the Holy Spirit for a greater measure. The Lord will use your dreams and visions to train you in these giftings and impart to you in a greater capacity. These revelatory giftings also represent realms of the prophetic. The more you understand the realms of the prophetic, the more you'll be able to navigate them in your night seasons.

Prayer Declaration

Holy Spirit, I desire a greater measure of the revelatory gifts in my life. Active these gifts in my life in my night season. Teach me how to navigate the realms of the prophetic through my dreams and visions in the night.

Word of Knowledge

For to one is given through the Spirit the utterance of wisdom, and

to another the utterance of knowledge according to the same Spirit.

1 Corinthians 12:8 ESV

What is a word of knowledge? A word of knowledge is information or a fact about a person or situation that God supernaturally reveals to you. This information is not known until the Spirit of God reveals it. We often see words of knowledge being released in a ministry situation when prophetic ministry is taking place. Words of knowledge are not subject just to a ministry moment. Words of knowledge can show up in your dreams and visions in the night.

I tend to receive words of knowledge in this manner. Words of knowledge can be a situation that someone is going through, it can be a phone number, God revealing a sickness one is dealing will, a talent some one may have, or a plot of the enemy the Lord reveals. Let me give you a couple examples. There was a leader in my life that I was walking close with for a season. In a dream, I had joined this leader at an event they were speaking at. As I was entering the sanctuary in the dream, I heard them singing the Word of the Lord over the people and the land. In real life, I had no idea they could sing or that the Lord used them in that way. I contacted the person about the dream, and they confirmed it was true- they can sing and the Lord uses them in that way at times.

Another example that is more serious is in a dream or vision of the night in February 2020, the Lord took me to a laboratory in China. The Lord showed me where the corona virus was made and engineered, and other things to come. The Lord gave me a word of knowledge to bring exposure to the plans of the enemy, and to know how to pray. Words of knowledge are an invitation to partner with the Holy Spirit.

Prayer Declaration

Holy Spirit, help me to grow in the things of the Spirit in a greater way. I ask for the increase of the gift of word of knowledge in my life, especially in my dreams and visions. Show me the hidden things so I can partner with you in a greater way in prayer and impacting those around me.

Word of Wisdom

For to one is given through the Spirit the utterance of wisdom, and

to another the utterance of knowledge according to the same Spirit.

1 Corinthians 12:8 ESV

The word of wisdom is a part of the prophetic realm that brings solutions. Often times when we receive a prophetic word or an instruction, we need the wisdom of God to see the fruit of those things come to pass. The word of wisdom gives us the council of the Lord and the steps we need to take so we can see the prophetic words and promises come to pass. Kenneth Hagin said it like this, *"The word of wisdom is a supernatural revelation by the Spirit of God concerning the divine purpose in the mind and will of God."*

In James 1:5 it says, *"If anyone lacks wisdom, he should ask God who gives generously to all without finding fault."* More than ever in the times we're living in we need the wisdom of God to navigate these end times. I'm reminded of the story of Joseph and the Pharaoh in Genesis 41. In this passage, the Pharaoh had a dream where he saw seven healthy cows well fed cows, then he saw seven other unhealthy and thin looking cows along the Nile River. The thin, sickly cows ate the healthy ones. He also had another dream after the first one of seven healthy heads of grain and seven thin grains of head. And like the first dream, the seven thin heads are the healthy plump heads of grain.

God gave Joseph the opportunity to interpret Pharaoh's dreams. The Lord was showing Pharaoh there would be seven years of abundance, followed by seven years of famine. Because the Lord gave Joseph the interpretation, the Pharaoh appointed Joseph over the land of Egypt. From the dream, Joseph was able to use the wisdom of God to plan accordingly and preserve the nation in the time of famine. God wants to do the same for you. His wisdom preserves us and helps us to victorious over what may come.

Prayer Declaration

Holy Spirit, I ask for more of your wisdom to fill my life. I need your wisdom and council to navigate and see the promises of God manifest in my life. As I sleep, release and impart your wisdom to my mind and spirit. I will not rely on my own understanding. I receive your council in my night season.

Prophecy

To another the working of miracles, to another prophecy, to another the ability to distinguish between spirits, to another various kinds of tongues, to another the interpretation of tongues.

1 Corinthians 12:10 ESV

Every believer has the capacity and ability to prophesy to some degree. Prophecy reveals the heart, mind, will and emotions of God. Did you know that you can release prophecy in a dream, or receive prophesy in a dream? Throughout the bible there are places where it says, *"and the Lord put him into a deep sleep."* It's in this place of sleep the Lord would reveal prophecy and prophesy to his people. Prophecy releases transformation because it contains the power to move us from one place in God to another. You may have gone to sleep one way, but as the prophecy was released in your night season you woke up shifted to a new place in your heart, mind, and spirit.

Before I stepped into full time ministry, I was a counseling therapist. There came a point where God began to prophesy my future in my dreams. He began to show me that he was calling me out of my career and into full time ministry. The prophetic word in my night season began to shift me in my spirit, mind, and will because I was seeing God's heart and desire for my life. Your dreams are prophecy. Sometimes we are looking for prophetic words from others, but all along God has been prophesying to you in your night season.

Prayer Declaration

Holy Spirit, speak your prophetic words over my life as sleep. I want to know your heart, mind, will, and emotions towards me. I posture my heart to receive your prophetic declarations spoken over my life. I receive prophetic words to prophesy to those around me and those who you show me in the night season. Increase the gift of prophecy in my life.

Discerning of Spirits

To another the working of miracles, to another prophecy, to another the ability to distinguish between spirits 1 Corinthians 12:10 ESV

But solid food is for the mature, whose spiritual senses perceive heavenly matters. And they have been adequately trained by what they've experienced to emerge with understanding of the difference between what is truly excellent and what is evil and harmful. Hebrews 5:14 TPT

Discerning of spirits is one of the greatest gifts and weapons the Lord has given us. We need to ask the Lord to increase our discernment. It's seeing in the supernatural. Discernment will save you from the plans of the enemy and people's wrong motives. Discernment helps us to discern the heart or the source of the matter. It reveals if something is godly, demonic, or flesh. Just as we can discern in the natural, or our awake state, we can discern in our night seasons. It's important to pay attention to these dreams. The more you trust what God is revealing, the more your discernment will mature and grow.

It's important to remember discernment is seeing through love. Love is able to rightly divide and judge. There have been times when I was needing discernment and to rightly see the situation, so I would ask God for a dream. There was a time when I was dealing with a lot of warfare, and I couldn't find the source. The enemy was trying to make it seem like it was me, but I knew it wasn't. It was something bigger. Before going to bed I asked God to give me a dream to show me what was going on. As I fell asleep, I fell into a trance. I suddenly found myself walking around my neighborhood in the daytime. I was walking past a fence when something caught my attention. Next thing I know a black cat came out of nowhere running full force at me getting ready to leap onto my chest and I woke up alarmed. Talk about the Lord revealing the plans of the enemy! Because of what the Lord revealed, I now know how to deal with it in the spirit realm.

There are also other times God will use our night seasons to reveal hearts. Sometimes it can be good, or sometimes God is revealing our heart and motives in a matter in order to deal with what's going on in us. And then there are times where God will show us in the night the hearts and motives of others. This can be shocking and hard to handle at times. I remember a time where the Lord gave me a dream about a leader in the body of Christ. In the dream, everything about them was the opposite of how they presented in the natural- even their attitude was different. I woke up from that encounter disturbed at what I saw. It's important to remember God doesn't reveal these things to expose people, but for us to go into prayer for them. Discerning of spirits is a powerful gift of the Spirit the Lord wants to activate in a great capacity in your night seasons.

Prayer Declaration

Holy Spirit, I ask for a greater measure of the gift of discerning of spirits. In my night season, teach me how to see in the supernatural through discernment. Teach me how to discern what's from you, the enemy, or the flesh. Help me to respond with maturity when you reveal the hidden things. I want to see through your eyes and heart.

Secrets

He reveals the deep and hidden things; he knows what is in the darkness, and light dwells with him. Daniel 2:22 CSB

I will give you the treasures of darkness and riches from secret places, so that you may know that I am the Lord. I am the God of Israel, who calls you by your name. Isaiah 45:3 CSB

For some reason, we have allowed the enemy to pervert and take over the darkness. We have feared going into the dark places because we believe that's where the enemy dwells. Did you know that it was God who first dwelled in the darkness? Psalm 18:11 says, *"He made darkness his hiding place, dark storm clouds his canopy around him."* We are used to experiencing God in the heights of Glory, but rarely are we willing to encounter God in the depths of glory. It's in the depths of His glory that He hides his secrets, treasures, and the deep things.

The night season is an invitation to encounter and experience the depths of God. There are certain things God cannot show you in the day. It can only be revealed in the dark place of His glory because the enemy cannot go there. His access has been denied, but our access has been granted because of the blood of Jesus. What else gives us access to this place? Being a friend of God. It's all about relationship. God will only share His most intimate secrets with those who have His heart.

Encounters in this place in God are so intimate. It's not something to be shared lightly. Treasure like this is not something you want to throw before the pigs (Matt 7:6). Cherish these intimate encounters in the night season. They will mark you and change you forever. Once you see His face, there's no turning back.

Prayer Declaration

Holy Spirit, as I go to sleep take me into the depths of who are. I want to experience you in the dark place of your glory. It says in your Word that you have stored up hidden treasures and riches from the darkness. You are the great revealer of mysteries and secrets.

Take me where I've never been before. I will cherish and guard

what you have showed me in the night, in the secret place.

Angels

You make your messengers into winds of the Spirit and all your

ministers become flames.

Psalm 104:4 TPT

Are they not all ministering spirits sent out to serve those who are

going to inherit salvation? Hebrews 1:14 CSB

Angels have always been a part of the story, too. The Bible is filled with stories of angels interacting with humans. I encourage you to look them up to learn more about them. There are many types and functions of angels. Some are specifically assigned to the throne of God and guarding His presence. Other angels war in the heavenlies, bring messages, assist us, bring breakthrough, harvest- the list could go on. As you encounter the Lord in your night season, don't be surprised if you start seeing and experiencing angels in your night season as well. How do you know if an angel/angels are among you? Ask the Holy Spirit for discernment. Here are some signs they may be among you- you feel fire, wind, you have a knowing or awareness of their presence, you can see them, you may find a feather. It's different for everyone.

If you want to become more aware of the angelic realm, ask the Holy Spirit to make you more sensitive and aware of their presence. In my night seasons, there are times I'm aware of angels at my bedside, sometimes triggering encounters, they assist me in dreams, they are present watching over my children as they sleep to guard against the attacks of the enemy. The ultimate goal of the angelic is not only to watch over us and assist us, but to help carry out the Word of the Lord to see it come to pass and be fulfilled. Don't be surprised if you start to notice more angelic activity since reading this. Often times we are entertaining angels unaware.

Prayer Declaration

Holy Spirit, awaken my senses and spirit to angelic activity. Thank you for your angels that you have sent to help me and minister to me. I declare and decree the angels of the Lord are assisting and watching over the Word of my life to see it come to fulfillment. Holy Spirit teach me how to interact and partner with the angelic in my night seasons.

Traveling In The Realm of The Spirit

He stretched out what looked like a hand and took me by the hair of my head. The Spirit lifted me up between earth and heaven and in visions of God he took me to Jerusalem, to the entrance of the north gate of the inner court, where the idol that provokes to jealousy stood. Ezekiel 8:3

In the night seasons, the more you learn to surrender yourself and let go, the more able the Spirit of God is able to take you places as you sleep. There are a couple different ways to travel in the Spirit. You can travel in your mind's eye, your spirit, or your body. Traveling in the Spirit is never initiated by us, but by the Spirit of God. When we travel within Holy Spirit, we are safe and protected.

Just as Ezekiel said the Spirit lifted me up, it's really that easy. It's nothing to be scared of. The Spirit of God wants to take you places that you cannot experience on earth. When we travel in the Spirit, we are able to do things in the Spirit we could not do in the natural. We are able to see from God's perspective. In my night seasons, I have found myself traveling all over the United States and different countries. God will often use these encounters to deal with demonic strongholds and principalities. God will take us in the Spirit to deal with the spirit of the matter in small and great circumstances.

Anything is possible with the Spirit. There are times he will send you to help those in need. One of the prayers I pray as I lay down is I ask God to use me or send me to those, even as I sleep, that need help. I will get messages or calls that I was in someone's dream assisting them. At times, the Spirit of God has taken me between the earth and space like Ezekiel. There have been times when the Spirit of God took me into Heaven. This is your portion too. Traveling in the Spirit is nothing to fear. I encourage you to look at the stories of Jesus and some of the other prophets who traveled in the Spirit. God wants to take you on new adventures in your night season. Are you ready?

Prayer Declaration

Holy Spirit, I want to travel in the realm of the Spirit. Take me where I've never been. I want to see things from your eyes and vantage. As I go to sleep, I once again surrender myself to you. I declare and decree I will not fear the places you take me. Send me to those in need. Teach me how to navigate the realms of the Spirit as we travel together.

Prophetic Sight

When there is no clear prophetic vision, people quickly wander

astray. But when you follow the revelation of the word, heaven's

bliss fills your soul. Proverbs 29:18 TPT

Prophet sight and vision is so important. Like the scripture says, when there is no clear prophetic vision, it's easy to go astray or get discouraged. The enemy wars over our vision because he knows the power of vision. That's why he will come in the night seasons to war against our dreams and visions because he wants to get us off course. I have gone through seasons where it seems like I can't "see" because my dreams are being fought or distorted. When you go through seasons like that, keep pressing through. Stay in the Word. When you can't see in the Spirit, His Word will be a lamp that will be revelation and light up your vision. God will often times use seasons like this to upgrade your vision.

One of the Hebrew words for the Seer is *chozeh*. One of the main meanings is beholder of vision. Ra'ah is another Hebrew word used in the seer realm. It means to see, have vision, to look at, or observe. It's important to be mindful at what we are beholding. What we behold we become. These encounters in our night seasons aren't meant just to be cool experiences. As we behold new and different levels of glory through the dreams and visions in the night, they are meant for us to become more like him, and to look more like him going from glory to glory. I'm reminded of Moses. Moses encountered God in such a way that he had to wear a veil on his face because the glory was so strong. May these encounters produce a glory and vision in your life that is undeniable.

Prayer Declaration

Holy Spirit, I need your prophetic vision for my life. I just don't want to have prophetic dreams and visions. I want to behold you. Because the more I behold you, the more I become like you and the vision you have for my life. I declare and decree what you have shown me in the dark, will become a reality in the day.

Prophetic Dreams

For God speaks in one way, and in two, though man does not

perceive it.¹⁵ In a dream, in a vision of the night, when deep sleep

falls on men, while they slumber on their beds,¹⁶ then he opens the

ears of men and terrifies them with warnings,¹⁷ that he may turn

man aside from his deed and conceal pride from a man.

Job 33:14-17 ESV

It is amazing what God can release to us in our night seasons. In Amos 3:7 it says, *"For the Lord God does nothing without revealing his secret to his servants the prophets."* That is such a powerful concept. Think about that for a moment. God will do nothing in the earth without first revealing it to one of his prophets. God doesn't have to do that, but he wants to include us.

He chooses to use us to be a conduit from Heaven to earth. As the saying goes, we can't without God, and He will not without us.

In this scripture in Job, it says the Lord speaks to us in multiple ways in our night seasons. When God speaks to us in multiple ways, He is bringing confirmation to His word and He desires to establish it in our lives. The Word says by two or three witnesses a thing is established (Matt 18:16). Pay attention to those dreams and encounters the Lord speaks to you in multiple ways. He is trying to get your attention, so you don't miss Him or fall into a trap of the enemy. I have found when I have a dream within a dream or a vision within in a dream, its imminent in coming to pass.

Dreams and visions are such a powerful tool of communication. Dreams are the language of Heaven. God wants to make himself known to you not just in the day but in your night seasons. He is such a big God, but also such a personal God. As you learn to steward your dreams and night encounters, you'll build a beautiful place of intimacy and communication in your night seasons.

Prayer Declaration

Holy Spirit, increase my prophetic dreams. Like the scripture in Job 33, speak to me in multiple ways. Establish your word and your promises through my night encounters with you. Give me greater understanding and clarity in my dreams and encounters. I don't want to miss what you're speaking to me. I want to build and grow my dream language. Speak to me in my night seasons. I'm listening and watching.

The Search

God conceals the revelation of his word in the hiding place of his

glory. But the honor of kings is revealed by how they thoroughly

search out the deeper meaning of all that God says. The heart of a

king is full of understanding, like the heavens are high and the

ocean is deep.   Proverbs 25:2-3 TPT

As your dreams and night encounters begin to increase, its important to not become too familiar or common with them. When we treat the things we once held as holy, common, it will shut off the flow. When we become too familiar with the way God speaks to us, we're not able to hear or receive from him like we used to. Never lose the wonder of how the Lord speaks to you in the night through dreams and encounters. How God speaks to you is a holy thing.

With each dream, vision, and encounter, God is hiding himself within each one. How willing or hungry are you to search out the greater meanings of your night encounters? I want to encourage you not to stop at the surface level revelation. Go deeper. Dreams and encounters have several layers of revelation to be uncovered. With each new discovery of understanding and revelation, a new glory is released. I'm reminded of the story of the parable of the man in Matthew 13. He discovered a treasure hidden in a field, and he sold everything he had to buy the field with the treasure.

May that be the posture of our hearts. The story also says that he hid it again after finding it. It wasn't that the man was ashamed of the treasure, he was guarding His revelation. I want to caution you as we close to be careful not to share every encounter. Some encounters are too personal and intimate to share. You don't want to throw your pearls before the swine. Learn to wear the treasures of your encounters instead of forfeiting them before those who will just trample on them and exploit them. Be slow to share your encounters. Cherish them. Don't pursue the glory of man. Pursue after the glory of God. He rewards those who diligently seek after Him.

Prayer Declaration

Holy Spirit, help me to never lose my wonder of pursuing after you. Forgive me for the times where I've become too familiar with the way you speak to me in the night. Help me to steward my dreams and encounters in the night. I want to wear them well. I will cherish these moments and the revelations you reveal in the night. I declare and decree I will pursue after you wholeheartedly.

Prayer of Impartation

Holy Spirit, I pray for those who have read this devotional, that the eyes of their heart be opened in a greater capacity than before. Increase their dreams, visions, and night encounters. For those who have been battling warfare in their night seasons, I command every attack of the enemy to break off of your life. I declare and decree that your sleep will be sweet and no longer tormented.

Holy Spirit, I impart to the readers everything that has been imparted to me concerning dreams, visions, and encounters. Give them greater wisdom, understanding, and revelation of their encounters. Teach them how to command their night seasons to walk in victory in the day. Increase the capacity of every reader so they can continue to grow and mature in the things of the Spirit. In Jesus

name, amen.